To ....

From ....

Date ....

The Bible Reading Fellowship
15 The Chambers, Vineyard
Abingdon OX14 3FE
brf.org.uk

The Bible Reading Fellowship (BRF) is a Registered Charity (233280)

ISBN 978 0 85746 524 5
First published 2016
10 9 8 7 6 5 4 3 2 1 0
All rights reserved

Cover image: *Eternal*, © Jenny Meehan. All rights reserved, DACS 2016

Acknowledgements
Scripture quotations taken from The Holy Bible, New International Version (Anglicised edition) copyright © 1979, 1984, 2011 by Biblica. Used by permission of Hodder & Stoughton Publishers, a Hachette UK company. All rights reserved. 'NIV' is a registered trademark of Biblica. UK trademark number 1448790.

Scripture quotations taken from The New Revised Standard Version of the Bible, Anglicised edition, copyright © 1989, 1995 by the Division of Christian Education of the National Council of the Churches of Christ in the United States of America. Used by permission. All rights reserved.

Scripture quotations taken from the Holy Bible, English Standard Version, published by HarperCollins Publishers, © 2001 Crossway Bibles, a division of Good News Publishers. Used by permission. All rights reserved.

Every effort has been made to trace and contact copyright owners for material used in this resource. We apologise for any inadvertent omissions or errors, and would ask those concerned to contact us so that full acknowledgement can be made in the future.

A catalogue record for this book is available from the British Library

Printed and bound by Gutenberg Press, Tarxien, Malta

Quiet Spaces
Prayer Journal

People I pray for regularly

YEAR TO VIEW ✒ *Significant dates or milestones*

JANUARY	FEBRUARY	MARCH	APRIL	MAY	JUNE

JULY	AUGUST	SEPTEMBER	OCTOBER	NOVEMBER	DECEMBER

YEAR TO VIEW ❧ *Significant dates or milestones*

Date ....

For God alone my soul waits in silence.
PSALM 62:1a, NRSV

Note down any thoughts that may distract you.

Date ....

_____

_____

_____

_____

_____

_____

_____

_____

_____

_____

_____

I wait for the Lord, my soul waits, and in his word I hope;
my soul waits for the Lord more than those who watch
for the morning.
PSALM 130:5–6a, NRSV

What am I waiting or hoping for?

....
....
....
....
....
....
....
....
....
....
....
....
....
....
....
....
....
....

Date ....

....

....

....

....

....

....

....

....

....

....

....

....

....

....

Do not worry about anything, but in everything
by prayer and supplication with thanksgiving
let your requests be made known to God.
PHILIPPIANS 4:6, NRSV

Write a list of worries and 'release' them to God.

Date ....

Thank you, Lord, for the gift of rest and sleep. Ahead of me lies
a fresh day, unblemished; may I be open to your voice through
your word, your Spirit, your people, creation and circumstances.
FIONA STRATTA

Review the day at its end.

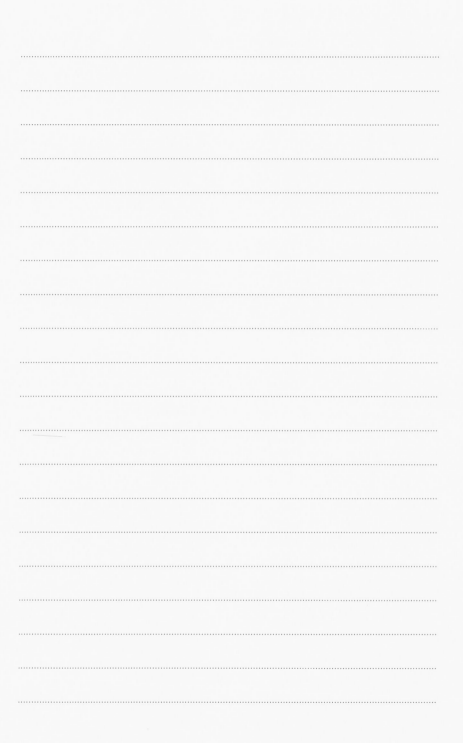

Date ....

My flesh and my heart may fail, but God is the strength
of my heart and my portion for ever.
PSALM 73:26, NIV

What am I apprehensive about?

Date ....

(ruled writing lines)

Here is love, vast as the ocean, loving kindness as the flood,
When the Prince of Life, our ransom, shed for us his precious blood.
WILLIAM REES (1802–83)

Perhaps you could sing or play this song.

Date ....

....

....

....

....

....

....

....

....

....

....

....

....

....

Search me, God, and know my heart;
test me and know my anxious thoughts.
See if there is any offensive way in me,
and lead me in the way everlasting.
PSALM 139:23–24, NIV

How do I see myself?

Date ....

_____

_____

_____

_____

_____

_____

_____

_____

_____

_____

_____

_____

_____

Be kind and compassionate to one another,
forgiving each other, just as in Christ God forgave you.
EPHESIANS 4:32, NIV

Is there anyone I need to forgive?

Date ....

....

....

....

....

....

....

....

....

....

....

....

....

....

Therefore I tell you, do not worry about your life, what you will eat
or what you will drink, or about your body, what you will wear.
Is not life more than food, and the body more than clothing?
MATTHEW 6:25, NRSV

How can I truly rest in God?

Date ....

....

....

....

....

....

....

....

....

....

....

....

....

....

....

....

....

....

....

....

....

....

'For I know the plans I have for you,' declares the Lord,
'plans to prosper you and not to harm you,
plans to give you hope and a future.'
JEREMIAH 29:11, NIV

What are my hopes for the future?

Date ....

....

....

....

....

....

....

....

....

....

....

....

....

....

....

Come, all you who are thirsty, come to the waters;
and you who have no money, come, buy and eat!
Isaiah 55:1, NIV

How can I share God's living water with others?

Date ....

....

....

....

....

....

....

....

....

....

....

....

....

....

....

Breathe on me, breath of God; fill me with life anew;
That I may love what thou dost love and do what thou wouldst do.
EDWIN HATCH (1835–89)

Help me to reach out to those in need.

Date ....

....

....

....

....

....

....

....

....

....

....

....

....

God is our refuge and strength, an ever-present help in trouble.
Therefore we will not fear, though the earth give way
and the mountains fall into the heart of the sea.
Psalm 46:1–2, NIV

When have I been afraid?

Date ....

....

....

....

....

....

....

....

....

....

....

....

....

....

....

....

....

....

....

Who is like you, Lord God Almighty?
You, Lord, are mighty, and your faithfulness surrounds you.
PSALM 89:8, NIV

Meditate on this verse in silence.

Date ....

....

....

....

....

....

....

....

....

....

....

....

....

....

....

....

Lord God, help me to believe this day that you are my light
and my salvation, my refuge and dwelling place. Amen
ANNE NOBLE

Light a candle.

Date ....

....

....

....

....

....

....

....

....

....

....

....

....

Christ has no body now on earth but yours.
Yours are the eyes through which he looks with compassion
on the world.
ATTRIBUTED TO ST TERESA OF AVILA (1515–82)

How can I respond?

Date ....

....

....

....

....

....

....

....

....

....

....

....

....

....

....

He did not say, 'You shall not be tormented, you shall not be troubled,
you shall not be grieved,' but he said, 'You shall not be overcome.'
JULIAN OF NORWICH (1342–1416)

Do I truly believe this?

Date ....

....

....

....

....

....

....

....

....

....

....

....

....

....

....

....

....

....

....

....

....

I praise you because I am fearfully and wonderfully made;
your works are wonderful, I know that full well.
PSALM 139:14, NIV

Tell another person how special they are.

Date ....

....

....

....

....

....

....

....

....

....

....

....

....

Love is patient and kind; love does not envy or boast;
it is not arrogant or rude. It does not insist on its own way;
it is not irritable or resentful; it does not rejoice at wrongdoing,
but rejoices with the truth.

1 Corinthians 13:4–7, ESV

How loving am I?

Date ....

....

....

....

....

....

....

....

....

....

....

....

....

....

....

....

Lord, help me to be alive to your glory in creation,
to be attentive to your voice in the actions of the day
and to see your face in the faces of those I meet.
SALLY WELCH

Meet with a friend to pray.

Date ....

....

....

....

....

....

....

....

....

....

....

....

....

....

....

Alone with none but thee, my God, I journey on my way.
What need I fear when thou art near, O king of night and day?
St Columba (c. 521–597)

'Journey' boldly into your community today.

Date ....

....

....

....

....

....

....

....

....

....

....

....

....

....

....

....

....

....

....

....

....

Take my yoke upon you and learn from me, for I am gentle
and humble in heart, and you will find rest for your souls.
For my yoke is easy and my burden is light.

MATTHEW 11:29–30, NIV

What have I learned today, or this week?

....
....
....
....
....
....
....
....
....
....
....
....
....
....
....
....
....

Date ....

....

....

....

....

....

....

....

....

....

....

....

....

....

....

....

....

....

....

Beloved, let us love one another, for love is from God,
and whoever loves has been born of God and knows God.
1 JOHN 4:7, ESV

Visit someone who is lonely.

Date ....

....

....

....

....

....

....

....

....

....

....

....

....

....

....

....

....

....

....

....

God, grant me the serenity to accept the things I cannot change,
courage to change the things I can,
and the wisdom to know the difference.

REINHOLD NIEBUHR (1892–1971)

Keep calm and dare with discernment!

Date ....

....

....

....

....

....

....

....

....

....

....

....

....

Carry each other's burdens, and in this way
you will fulfil the law of Christ.
GALATIANS 6:2, NIV

How could I do this for a friend?

Date ....

....

....

....

....

....

....

....

....

....

....

....

....

Gracious God, bless our hands with the gift of gentleness,
our hearts with the gift of compassion and our eyes
with the love to see you at work in all places.
LYNNE CHITTY

Speak, move and act gently and kindly today.

Date ....

Earth's crammed with heaven,
And every common bush afire with God.
ELIZABETH BARRETT BROWNING (1806–61)

Take a photo or draw a picture of something beautiful.

....

....

....

....

....

....

....

....

....

....

....

....

....

....

....

....

Date ....

....

....

....

....

....

....

....

....

....

....

....

....

....

....

....

God loves each of us as if there were only one of us.
ST AUGUSTINE OF HIPPO (354–430)

Look at yourself in a mirror and repeat these words.

Date ....

....

....

....

....

....

....

....

....

....

....

....

....

....

Lord, make me an instrument of thy peace.
Where there is hatred, let me sow love.
ATTRIBUTED TO ST FRANCIS OF ASSISI (1182–1226)

How can I make a difference?

Date ....

....

....

....

....

....

....

....

....

....

....

....

....

....

....

....

....

Be thou my vision, O Lord of my heart;
naught be all else to me, save that thou art;
Thou my best thought, by day or by night;
waking or sleeping, thy presence my light.
ATTRIBUTED TO DALLÁN FORGAILL (SIXTH CENTURY)

Listen to some uplifting music.

Date ....

....

....

....

....

....

....

....

....

....

....

....

....

....

....

....

....

The steadfast love of the Lord never ceases,
his mercies never come to an end;
they are new every morning;
great is your faithfulness.
LAMENTATIONS 3:22–23, NRSV

Claim this promise for even the hardest of situations.

Date ....

I saw that God is our true peace; and he is our safe protector
when we ourselves are in disquiet, and he constantly works
to bring us into endless peace.

JULIAN OF NORWICH (1342–1416)

Pray for peace in our communities, locally, nationally and internationally.

Date ....

_____

_____

_____

_____

_____

_____

_____

_____

_____

_____

_____

_____

One thing I ask from the Lord, this only do I seek:
that I may dwell in the house of the Lord all the days of my life,
to gaze on the beauty of the Lord and to seek him in his temple.
PSALM 27:4, NIV

Where do I feel closest to God?

Date ....

Ask, and it will be given to you; search, and you will find;
knock, and the door will be opened for you.
Luke 11:9, NRSV

What am I seeking at the moment?

Date ....

....

....

....

....

....

....

....

....

....

....

....

....

....

....

How lovely is your dwelling place, O Lord of hosts!
My soul longs, yes, faints for the courts of the Lord;
my heart and flesh sing for joy to the living God.
PSALM 84:1–2, ESV

What gives me joy?

Date ....

....

....

....

....

....

....

....

....

....

....

....

....

I am sure that neither death nor life, nor angels nor rulers,
nor things present nor things to come, nor powers, nor height
nor depth, nor anything else in all creation, will be able to
separate us from the love of God in Christ Jesus our Lord.
ROMANS 8:38–39, ESV

Write out this verse and keep it with you.

Date ....

Peace I leave with you; my peace I give you.
I do not give to you as the world gives.
Do not let your hearts be troubled and do not be afraid.

JOHN 14:27, NIV

What am I struggling with right now?

Date ....

....

....

....

....

....

....

....

....

....

....

....

....

....

....

....

....

The stillness of winter, the wonder of spring, the joys of summer,
the fruitfulness of autumn, for these we thank you, Lord.

FIONA STRATTA

Reflect on the blessings of the current season.

....

....

....

....

....

....

....

....

....

....

....

....

....

....

....

....

Date ....

....

....

....

....

....

....

....

....

....

....

....

....

....

....

He has told you, O mortal, what is good;
and what does the Lord require of you but to do justice,
and to love kindness, and to walk humbly with your God?
MICAH 6:8, NRSV

What are the challenges of this?

Date ....

....

....

....

....

....

....

....

....

....

....

....

....

Trust in the Lord and do good;
dwell in the land and enjoy safe pasture.
Take delight in the Lord, and he will give you
the desires of your heart.
PSALM 37:3–4, NIV

What are the desires of my heart?

....

....

....

....

....

....

....

....

....

....

....

....

....

....

....

Date ....

....

....

....

....

....

....

....

....

....

....

....

....

....

Trust in the Lord with all your heart
and lean not on your own understanding;
in all your ways submit to him,
and he will make your paths straight.
PROVERBS 3:5–6, NIV

Is there something I need to change?

Date ....

I am the light of the world. Whoever follows me
will never walk in darkness, but will have the light of life.
JOHN 8:12b, NIV

Gather together different sources of light and shine them in the darkness.

....

....

....

....

....

....

....

....

....

....

....

....

....

....

Date ....

_____

_____

_____

_____

_____

_____

_____

_____

_____

_____

_____

_____

The grass withers and the flowers fall,
but the word of our God endures for ever.
ISAIAH 40:8, NIV

If you can, go for a walk outside.

Date ....

....

....

....

....

....

....

....

....

....

....

....

....

....

....

....

Let nothing disturb you, let nothing frighten you.
All things pass away: God never changes.
ST TERESA OF AVILA (1515–82)

Find a way to encourage someone today.

Date ....

....
....
....
....
....
....
....
....
....
....
....
....
....
....
....
....

Be still, and know that I am God
Be still and know that I am
Be still and know
Be still
Be

BASED ON PSALM 46:10a

For your insights and reflections as you look back through this journal

Published three times a year, each issue of *Quiet Spaces* provides four months' worth of inspiration for your quiet time, presented in fortnightly sections. This material can be used in daily portions throughout the week or all in one sitting as a Quiet Day, perhaps at the weekend. Within each section there are twelve elements comprising reflections inspired by different traditions, creative activities, liturgy, Bible reading and ideas for meditation.

Quiet Spaces
A creative response to God's love
Edited by Sally Smith

brfonline.org.uk